Make·It·In A Muffin Tin!

Meals, Snacks & Desserts

D1055788

Make-It-In A Muffin Tin
©Product Concept Mfg., Inc.

"How very clever!"

That's what your family members and friends will say when they realize the simple technique you used to create these tasty individual servings of entrees, side dishes, appetizers and desserts.

From saucy meatballs to Mexican Chicken Pinwheels, Crispy Apple Tarts to Vanilla-Toffee Mini Cheesecakes, you'll find all kinds of recipe ideas—all made right in a muffin tin! Oh, and many recipes are perfect to use a portion now, and store several servings in the freezer for a grab-and-go snack or lunch for another day.

You'll see how simple it can be to make a great dish...right in a muffin tin!

Table of Contents

. . . .

Table of Contents

· · · · · · · · · · · · · · · · · · ·

BREAKFAST IN A BASKET

Ingredients:
1 bag frozen shredded potatoes, thawed
4 Tbsp melted butter
6 large eggs
Cheddar cheese, finely shredded (optional)
6 bacon strips, cooked but still pliable

Directions:
Preheat oven to 350°. Spray a standard size muffin tin with non-stick cooking spray. Thaw the shredded potatoes and pour the melted butter over them, mixing well. Divide the potatoes among the muffin cups and press to the bottom and sides of the muffin cups. Bake in the oven for about 12 minutes until golden brown - watch closely so they don't burn. Remove from oven and lightly spray again with cooking spray. Break an egg into each potato basket. Bake for another 12 minutes or until the eggs are done to your preference. Gently remove the hash brown baskets from the muffin cups with a spoon or spatula. Sprinkle with shredded cheeses if desired. Put a piece of bacon from one side of the hash brown cup up and over like a handle to the other side. Adhere it with a toothpick if needed.

EGG MUFFIN CUPS

Ingredients:
6 slices hearty whole wheat bread
Butter, softened
6 slices Canadian bacon
6 large eggs
Salt and pepper

Directions:
Preheat oven to 350°. Spray a large size, 6-well muffin tin with non-stick cooking spray. Cut crusts off the bread slices and spread butter on both sides. Gently push each piece of bread into a muffin cup so that the center of the bread is down in the cup and the edges are hanging out of the cup. Place one slice of Canadian bacon in each cup and then break an egg into each cup. Sprinkle each egg with salt and pepper and bake in the oven for about 12-13 minutes or until egg is done to your liking.

WINTER MORNING OATMEAL BAKE

Ingredients:
1 egg
1 tsp vanilla extract
1 cup unsweetened applesauce
1 banana, mashed
1/4 cup honey
3 cups old-fashioned rolled oats
1 Tbsp cinnamon
1 1/2 tsp baking powder
1/2 tsp salt
1 1/2 cups whole milk
Optional toppings: blueberries, raisins, walnuts, chocolate
    chips, pomegranate seeds.

Directions:
Preheat oven to 350°. Spray a standard size muffin tin with
non-stick cooking spray. In a mixing bowl, combine the egg,
vanilla, applesauce, banana and honey. Add in oats, cinnamon,
baking powder, salt and mix well. Stir in the milk. Divide the
mixture evenly into muffin tin cups. Add the toppings you
prefer, and bake for 30 minutes or until a toothpick inserted
into the center comes out clean.

ON-THE-GO EGG MUFFINS

Ingredients:
Tomatoes, chopped
Green onion, chopped
Cheddar cheese, shredded
Green chiles
Fresh coriander
6 Eggs, beaten with 2 Tbsp milk
Salt and pepper to taste
Cooked chicken or other lean meats; spinach, ricotta cheese,
bell peppers, or whatever else you'd like to add

Directions:
Preheat oven to 350°. Spray a standard size muffin tin with
non-stick cooking spray. Put your choice of vegetables, cheese,
and meat into each muffin tin cup. Pour the beaten egg
mixture into each cup on top of the other ingredients. Place
muffin pan on the center rack and bake for 20-25 minutes or
until they are light brown, puffy, and the eggs are set. Let the
egg muffins cool for a few minutes before removing from the
muffin pan. Loosen gently with knife if they seem to be
sticking. Eat immediately or let cool completely and store
in plastic bag in refrigerator or freezer. The Egg Muffins
can be reheated in the microwave.

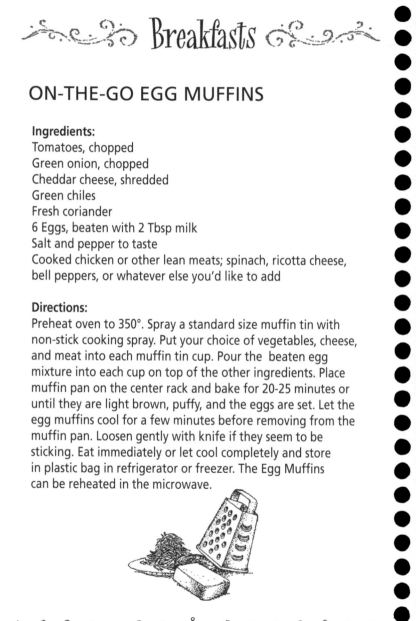

OVERNIGHT PECAN STICKY ROLLS

Ingredients:
Chopped pecans
Frozen dinner rolls (balls of dough)
1 pkg dry butterscotch pudding mix (not instant)
1/2-3/4 cup butter
1/2 cup brown sugar

Directions:
Spray a jumbo size muffin tin with non-stick cooking spray. Sprinkle pecans in the bottom of each muffin cup. Place 3 rolls in each cup. Sprinkle the dry pudding mix evenly over the tops of the frozen rolls. In a small saucepan, melt the butter and add the brown sugar, stirring until dissolved. Cool and then pour over the rolls. Cover with a clean dish towel and let rise overnight (not in the oven).

Preheat oven to 350°. Bake for 30 minutes or until golden brown. Gently remove each roll from the tin. There will be extra caramel sauce in each muffin cup—spoon that sauce over each roll until completely covered.

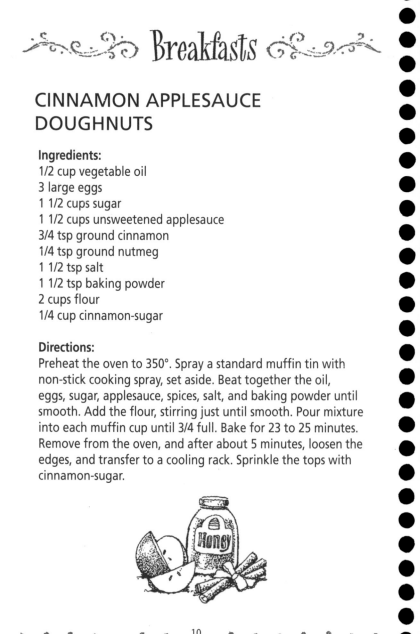

Breakfasts

CINNAMON APPLESAUCE DOUGHNUTS

Ingredients:
1/2 cup vegetable oil
3 large eggs
1 1/2 cups sugar
1 1/2 cups unsweetened applesauce
3/4 tsp ground cinnamon
1/4 tsp ground nutmeg
1 1/2 tsp salt
1 1/2 tsp baking powder
2 cups flour
1/4 cup cinnamon-sugar

Directions:
Preheat the oven to 350°. Spray a standard muffin tin with non-stick cooking spray, set aside. Beat together the oil, eggs, sugar, applesauce, spices, salt, and baking powder until smooth. Add the flour, stirring just until smooth. Pour mixture into each muffin cup until 3/4 full. Bake for 23 to 25 minutes. Remove from the oven, and after about 5 minutes, loosen the edges, and transfer to a cooling rack. Sprinkle the tops with cinnamon-sugar.

GRANOLA CUPS

Ingredients:
2/3 cup butter
1/4 cup honey
1 tsp vanilla extract
1/4 tsp almond extract
1/2 cup pecans, chopped
1/2 cup wheat germ
3 cups old fashioned oats
3/4 cup coconut
1/2 cup oat bran
1/2 cup brown sugar
1 tsp allspice
1 tsp cinnamon
Dried fruit: apricots, cranberries, bananas, apples, etc.
Choice of toppings, such as yogurt, ice cream, fruit, etc.

Directions:
Preheat oven to 350°. Spray a standard tin with non-stick cooking spray, set aside. In a medium saucepan, combine the honey and butter, stirring until melted. Add in the vanilla and almond extracts. In a large bowl combine all the dry ingredients. Pour the honey butter mix over all and stir well. Put a scoop of granola into each muffin cup and then, using your fingers, press onto the sides and bottom of the muffin cups, making a granola "cup". Bake for 15-20 minutes or until edges begin to turn brown. Remove from oven and let cool. Gently lift out of the muffin tin to a serving platter. Spoon fresh fruit, yogurt, ice cream, or pudding into each granola cup just before serving.

MINI VEGGIE QUICHE

Ingredients:
8 butter flavored crackers, finely crushed
1/4 cup Swiss cheese, shredded
2 cups fresh broccoli florets, chopped fine
1 cup fresh tomatoes, diced
1 cup corn
1 cup sweet red pepper, chopped fine
1/2 cup green onions, chopped fine
1 Tbsp olive oil
8 large eggs, beaten
Salt and pepper to taste
3/4 cup Cheddar cheese, shredded

Directions:
Preheat oven to 350°. Spray a standard size muffin tin with non-stick cooking spray, set aside. Mix together cracker crumbs and Swiss cheese in small bowl; set aside. Sauté broccoli and the other vegetables in the olive oil until tender then spoon into muffin tin cups. Add the cracker crumb mixture, the eggs, and salt and pepper. Top with the Cheddar cheese. Bake 18 to 22 minutes or until toothpick inserted in centers comes out clean.

SUNDAY MORNING EGGS

Ingredients:
3 English muffins, split and toasted
6 slices of Muenster cheese
6 slices Canadian bacon
1 fresh tomato, sliced into thin rounds
1 ripe avocado, sliced thin (optional)
1 dozen eggs
Salt and pepper to taste
3/4 cup sour cream
3/4 cup mayonnaise
1 Tbsp cream
1 Tbsp lemon juice
1 Tbsp Dijon mustard

Directions:
Preheat oven to 350°. Spray a jumbo size muffin tin with non-stick cooking spray. Place one half of an English muffin in each of the six muffin cups. Next, layer one slice of cheese, a slice of Canadian bacon, a slice of tomato, and a couple of slices of avocado if desired. Carefully break two eggs into each muffin cup, sprinkle with salt and pepper. Bake for 20 minutes or until eggs are baked to desired doneness.

While eggs are baking, make the sauce. In a small mixing bowl, combine the sour cream, mayonnaise, cream, lemon juice, and mustard. Whisk until completely combined, refrigerate until ready to use. Warm the sauce before pouring over cooked eggs.

Breakfasts

OVERNIGHT EGG DISH

Ingredients:
1 loaf French bread, sliced thick
2 cups Colby Jack cheese, shredded
2 cups cooked ham, cut into bite size pieces
1 cup asparagus spears, cooked and cut into 1-inch pieces
6 eggs, beaten
1/4 cup whole milk
Salt and pepper to taste

Directions:
Spray a jumbo muffin tin with non-stick cooking spray, set aside. Using a 3-inch round cookie cutter, cut out 12 rounds of bread. Place one round of bread in the bottom of the six muffin cups (saving the other 6 for the tops). Divide half of the cheese, ham, and asparagus among the muffin cups. Put another piece of bread on top of each. In a medium bowl, combine the eggs and milk and then pour it evenly over the bread. Using a spoon, press down on the bread to insure that it is moistened. Put the remaining cheese, ham, and asparagus on top and cover the pan with foil. Refrigerate overnight. In the morning, preheat the oven to 350°. Remove the foil and sprinkle the dish with salt and pepper. Bake for 30 minutes. Let set for about 5 minutes. Run a knife around the edges, then invert onto a serving platter.

PROTEIN PACKED ANYTIME MUFFINS

Ingredients:
3 Tbsp canola oil
3 Tbsp sugar
3 Tbsp honey
3 Tbsp peanut butter
1 egg
1 1/2 cups oat flour
1/2 cup quick cooking oats
1 tsp baking powder
1/4 tsp salt
1/2 cup whole milk
1/3 cup quinoa, cooked and cooled
1/2 cup chocolate chips

Directions:
Preheat the oven to 350°. Spray a standard muffin tin with non-stick cooking spray. Using an electric mixer, combine the oil, sugar, honey and peanut butter. Beat in the egg. In a bowl, combine the oat flour, instant oats, baking powder and salt. Add these dry ingredients to the egg and oil mixture a little at a time, alternating with the milk.

Fold in the cooked quinoa and chocolate chips. Bake at 350° for 20-25 minutes or until a toothpick inserted in the centers comes out clean.

Breakfasts

PANCAKES IN A MUFFIN TIN

Ingredients:
1/2 cup milk
1/2 cup flour
3 eggs
2 Tbsp butter, melted
Butter
Powdered sugar
Cinnamon
Fruit

Directions:
Preheat oven to 400°. Spray a standard size muffin tin with non-stick cooking spray. Put all ingredients into a blender and mix until smooth. Pour the mixture into the muffin tins. Bake them for 15 minutes, or until puffy and golden on top. Remove from muffin pan and cool slightly. Top with butter, syrup, powdered sugar, cinnamon, and/or fruit.

PEANUT BUTTER, BANANA AND CHOCOLATE SMOOTHIE

Ingredients:
2 bananas
1 cup creamy peanut butter
3/4 cup chocolate breakfast powder
1 1/2 cups unsweetened vanilla almond milk
1 cup vanilla yogurt
Chocolate syrup

Directions:
Add all of the ingredients to a blender or food processor. Blend until smooth. Pour into muffin tin cups and freeze. When ready to make, place one smoothie "muffin" into the blender with about 6 ice cubes. Blend until smooth, adding additional milk until desired consistency. Drizzle chocolate syrup on the insides of the glasses and then pour smoothie in. Enjoy!

OVER THE MOON CRAB CRESCENTS

Ingredients:
1 8-oz. tube crescent roll dough
3 oz. cream cheese, softened
1/4 cup mayonnaise
3/4 cup cooked crabmeat or crab substitute, chopped

Dipping sauce:
2 stalks of celery, finely chopped
2 green onions, finely chopped
1 tsp hot sauce or cocktail sauce
Salt and pepper to taste

Directions:
Preheat oven to 350°. Spray a standard size muffin tin with non-stick cooking spray. Roll out the tube of dough on a flat, slightly floured surface and pinch together the seams to form one large rectangle. Using a pizza cutter, cut the dough into about 3 inch squares. Mix the cream cheese, mayonnaise and crabmeat together. Place a spoonful of crab mixture in the middle of each square. Pull the corners up to the center and pinch together. Put each crab bite into a muffin tin cup and bake for 12-15 minutes or until golden. Mix dipping sauce ingredients together to make a tasty sauce.

NACHOS EXTRAORDINAIRE

Ingredients:
12 unbleached natural tulip baking cups, 2 1/2" x 4"
   (found online or in specialty baking shops)
1 large bag of tortilla chips
1 lb. hamburger
1/2 cup onion, chopped
1 can refried beans
1 pkg taco seasoning
1 cup salsa
Cheddar cheese, shredded
Sour cream
Avocado
Salsa

Directions:
Preheat the oven to 350°. Place the baking cups into the wells of two jumbo size muffin tins. Divide the chips into each baking cup, leaving room in the center for the other ingredients. In a medium frying pan, scramble the hamburger and onion together. Drain the grease off and add the refried beans, taco seasoning, and salsa. Stir together, cooking over medium heat for 3-5 minutes until very hot. Remove from heat. Put 1/4 cup of the meat/bean mixture in the center of each baking cup (on top of the chips), then cover with the shredded cheese. Bake in the oven for 7-10 minutes until cheese has melted. Serve with sour cream, avocado, and salsa on the side.

SAUCY MEATBALL APPETIZER

Ingredients:
2 homemade or refrigerated pie crusts
1 8-oz. package frozen cooked Italian style meatballs,
    mostly thawed
2 cups of homemade spaghetti sauce or 1 16-oz. jar of
    spaghetti sauce
Mozzarella cheese, shredded

Directions:
Preheat oven to 350°. Spray a standard size muffin tin
with non-stick cooking spray, set aside. Soften pie crusts
(if refrigerated) and, using a 6-inch circle cutter or a plate as
a template, cut out one round for each muffin cup. Center
the rounds in the muffin cups and gently press into each cup.
Place one meatball into each muffin cup and then a spoonful
of sauce to cover. Top with mozzarella cheese. Bake for 10-12
minutes until meatballs are hot and cheese has melted.

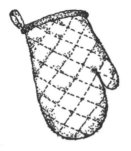

SPINACH ARTICHOKE APPETIZER

Ingredients:
1/2 cup Parmesan cheese, divided
16 oz. Mozzarella cheese, divided
1 can (8-oz.) refrigerated crescent dinner rolls
1 box (10-oz.) frozen creamed spinach
8 oz. cream cheese, softened
1/2 cup sour cream
1/2 cup mayonnaise
1/2 tsp minced garlic
1/2 tsp minced onion
1 cup marinated artichoke hearts, drained, sliced
Salt and pepper to taste

Directions:
Preheat oven to 375°. Spray 24 mini muffin cups with non-stick cooking spray. Put a mixture of the two cheeses, enough to make about 1/2 cup, in a small bowl. Reserve the remainder. Roll out the crescent roll dough into one large rectangle and then cut into 3-inch squares. Put one square of dough into each muffin tin well. Make spinach as directed on box. In a mixing bowl combine the cream cheese, sour cream, mayonnaise, garlic and onion and mix well. Stir in the artichoke hearts and the spinach. Season with salt and pepper. Put one spoonful of the spinach mixture into each dough square. Sprinkle the tops with the reserved cheeses. Bake for about 10-12 minutes until golden brown.

CORNY CORN-DOG BITES

Ingredients:
1 package corn muffin mix
1 large egg
1/2 cup buttermilk
1/2 cup frozen (thawed) or canned corn
1/4 cup sugar
6 hot dogs, cut into 1-inch pieces

Directions:
Preheat oven to 350°. Spray a mini size muffin tin with non-stick cooking spray. In a large bowl, combine the muffin mix, the egg, buttermilk, corn and sugar, stirring just until moist. Put one spoonful of batter into each cup and place 1 hot dog piece into the center. Bake for 8-10 minutes, or until golden brown. Remove from oven and cool on a wire rack.

Substitution hint: No buttermilk? Pour a scant 1/2 cup of regular milk into a measuring cup, add 2 teaspoons vinegar, and let set 5-10 minutes.

CREAMY APPLE APPETIZERS

Ingredients:
1 tube crescent roll dough
1 8-oz. package cream cheese
1/2 cup mayonnaise
1/2 cup shredded Cheddar cheese
3/4 cup apples, chopped fine
Honey, to taste
Dash of cinnamon

Directions:
Preheat oven to 350°. Unroll the dough and cut into 12 squares. Press one dough square into each of the muffin cups in a mini muffin pan. Using weights in each muffin cup, so that the dough stays formed as a crust, bake the dough until golden about 10 minutes. In a mixing bowl, combine the cream cheese and mayonnaise. Fold in the Cheddar cheese and apples. Add honey and cinnamon to your taste. Spoon into the warm pastry crusts and serve immediately.

Baking weights: When you need to bake a pie crust before filling it, it's called "blind baking". There are several ways to blind bake a pie or muffin tin crust. One suggestion is to put a disposable cupcake liner in each unbaked crust and fill with uncooked beans or rice. This gives it weight so the crust doesn't puff up and then fall. You can also use beans or rice wrapped in foil.

SMOKED SALMON SAMPLERS

Ingredients:
1 cup butter-flavored cracker crumbs
2 Tbsp butter, melted
1/2 cup onion, finely chopped
3 Tbsp butter
4 3-oz. packages cream cheese, softened
1/2 cup heavy whipping cream
1/4 cup Parmesan cheese
4 eggs
6 oz. smoked salmon, diced
2/3 cup Swiss cheese, shredded
Salt and pepper to taste

Directions:
Preheat oven to 325°. Spray a standard size muffin tin with non-stick cooking spray. In a bowl, combine the cracker crumbs and melted butter. Spoon into the muffin pan cups and press around the sides and bottoms to form crusts. Set aside. In a skillet, sauté the onion in butter until tender. Using an electric mixer, beat the cream cheese for 2 minutes until light and fluffy. Add in the cream, and Parmesan cheese. Add the eggs, one at a time, beating well after each. Stir in the onion, salmon, and Swiss cheese. Add salt and pepper to taste. Pour salmon mixture into the muffin cups about half full. Place the muffin tin in a larger baking dish and fill the large baking dish with about 1 inch of water to make a water-bath. Bake for 25-30 minutes until centers are almost set. Cool and then refrigerate. Loosen the crusts around the sides of each muffin cup with a knife and then lift out onto a platter. Serve with an assortment of crackers.

Appetizers

SURPRISING FIZZY PARTY DRINKS

Ingredients:
1 pint pineapple or orange sherbet, softened
1 box orange or lemon fizzie drink tablets
  (specialty candy stores or online)
Your favorite lemon-lime soda

Directions:
Spray a mini muffin tin with non-stick cooking spray. Spoon the softened sherbet into the muffin cups about half way. Put a fizzie tablet in each and cover it completely with more sherbet. Freeze until completely solid - at least overnight. When ready to serve, pour glasses of lemon-lime soda and spoon a sherbet "muffin" into each glass. If needed, loosen the sherbet by sliding a knife around the edges of the muffin cups and spooning out.

LITTLE SHRIMP TIDBITS

Ingredients:
Pie crust dough, cut into rounds
1 16-oz. container of cottage cheese
1/4 cup green onion, finely chopped
1–2 Tbsp spicy cocktail sauce (to taste)
2 Tbsp sour cream
2 Tbsp mayonnaise
Salt and pepper
1/2 cup small-medium cooked shrimp, diced
12 medium cooked shrimp, tail on

Directions:
Preheat the oven to 350°. Place one dough round in each of the muffin cups in a mini muffin tin. Using baking weights (see hint on page 23), bake the crusts for 10 minutes or until edges are golden. In the bowl of a food processor, combine the cottage cheese, onion, cocktail sauce, sour cream and mayonnaise. Blend until creamy. Add salt and pepper to taste. Stir in the chopped shrimp and then spoon the mixture into the pastry crusts. Place one whole shrimp on the top of each hors d'oeuvre. Serve chilled.

 Entrees

MINI BACON-CHEESEBURGERS

Ingredients:
6 soft dinner rolls, cut in half
1 lb. lean ground beef
1 medium onion, chopped
1/2 lb. bacon, cut into small pieces
1 Tbsp Worcestershire sauce
1 Tbsp barbeque sauce
1/2 tsp hot sauce (optional)
1 cup Cheddar cheese, shredded

Directions:
Preheat oven to 350°. Spray a jumbo size muffin tin with
non-stick cooking spray. Separate the rolls and place the
bottom half of each into the bottom of the muffin tin.
In a medium frying pan, scramble the hamburger and sauté
the chopped onion and bacon pieces until bacon is cooked
completely. Stir in the sauces while the meat is cooking.
Drain grease from pan. Add the shredded cheese to the meat
mixture, stirring to combine. Using an ice-cream scoop or a
large serving spoon, place one scoop of meat mixture onto
each bun. Top with the other half of each bun. Cover with foil
and bake for 10-12 minutes. Remove from oven and gently
set each mini-bacon cheeseburger onto a platter. Serve with
lettuce, sliced tomatoes, catsup, mustard, and pickles.

Entrees

INDIVIDUAL MEATLOAVES

Ingredients:
1 cup ketchup
3 Tbsp brown sugar
1 tsp mustard
2 eggs, lightly beaten
4 tsp Worcestershire sauce
1 cup dry oatmeal
1/2 cup onion, chopped fine
1/2 to 1 tsp seasoned salt
1/2 tsp garlic powder
1/2 tsp pepper
2 lbs. ground beef

Directions:
Preheat oven to 350°. In a large bowl, combine the ketchup, brown sugar and mustard. Remove 1/2 cup for topping; set aside. Add the eggs, Worcestershire sauce, oatmeal and seasonings to ketchup mixture. Crumble beef into these ingredients and mix well. Divide meat equally into the muffin cups. Bake for 18-20 minutes (shorter time for smaller meatloaves). Spread reserved ketchup mixture on top of each meatloaf and bake 10 minutes longer or until meat is no longer pink inside and a meat thermometer reads 160°.

Hint: You may want to use a mini muffin pan if it is for children or to make this recipe as an appetizer, or use a jumbo muffin tin if it is to be the main entree for a hungry bunch.

Entrees

MINI CHICKEN POT-PIES

Ingredients:
2 Tbsp butter
1/2 cup onion, finely chopped
1 cup baby carrots, sliced thin
2 tubes of large size biscuits (refrigerated dough)
1 cup cooked chicken breast, diced
1 (10 1/2-oz.) can cream of chicken soup
1/4 cup whole milk
1 cup frozen peas
1 cup Cheddar cheese, shredded
1/2 tsp poultry seasoning
1 tsp dried parsley flakes
Salt and pepper to taste

Directions:
Preheat oven to 400°. Spray a standard size muffin tin with non-stick cooking spray. In a frying pan, melt the butter and sauté the onion and carrots until tender.

Separate biscuits from one tube and place into muffin cups, pressing dough up sides and around the edges of the cup. Separate the biscuits in the second tube and cut out circles or stars or crowns using a cookie cutter then set aside. In a medium bowl, stir together the chicken, chicken soup, milk, sauteed veggies, peas, cheddar cheese, and spices. Mix well to combine. Evenly spoon chicken mixture into biscuit cups. Place one of the cut out shapes on the top of the chicken mixture in each cup. Bake for 12 to 15 minutes or until golden brown.

Hint: Fun shaped mini cookie cutters make special dough toppers for these little pot pies.

Entrees

EASY SAUSAGE AND RICE CUPS

Ingredients:
1 lb. Italian sausage
1 cup fresh mushrooms, sliced
1/2 cup celery, sliced
1/2 cup onion, chopped fine
1/2 cup slivered almonds
1 can (10 3/4-oz.) condensed cream of mushroom soup
2 cups water
1/4-1/2 cup quick cooking rice, to taste

Directions:
Preheat oven to 350°. Spray a standard size muffin tin with non-stick cooking spray. In a frying pan scramble the Italian sausage over medium heat. Drain the grease. Add the mushrooms, celery, onions, and slivered almonds, sautéing until tender. In a mixing bowl, whisk together the soup and 2 cups water. Add the sausage mixture to the soup, then add the rice. Spoon into the prepared muffin tin cups. Bake for 20-25 minutes or until set and lightly browned. Remove from oven and cool slightly before serving.

 Entrees

LASAGNA ROLLS

Ingredients:
1 large jar or about 8 cups prepared spaghetti sauce
1/2 lb. lean ground beef or Italian sausage, cooked and drained
1 10-oz. tub cream cheese or Herb & Cheese Cooking Cream
1/3 cup ricotta cheese
1/3 cup grated Parmesan cheese
3/4 lb. Mozzarella cheese, grated & divided
Salt and pepper to taste
1 egg
1 box of lasagna noodles

Directions:
Preheat oven to 350°. Spray two jumbo size muffin tins with non-stick cooking spray. Combine the browned meat and the spaghetti sauce, set aside. In another bowl, combine the cream cheese, ricotta, Parmesan and Mozzarella cheeses. Add the salt and pepper and egg, mixing well. Set aside. Bring a large pot of water to a boil. Cook pasta for about 2 minutes less than the package directions. It should be flexible but firm. Drain and pat dry with a paper towel. Lay each piece on a greased cookie sheet. Spoon a tablespoon of sauce onto each lasagna noodle, spread it out evenly, adding more sauce if needed. Next, spread a layer of the cheese mixture, then lay another lasagna noodle on top. Repeat the layering one more time, ending with a noodle. Begin carefully rolling one end of the layered noodle, holding steady to keep the sauce and cheese in. Lift very gently with a spatula and slide into a muffin cup. Top with more sauce and mozzarella cheese. Bake for 25-30 minutes.

MACARONI AND CHEESE WITH HAM

Ingredients:
6 pieces of thinly sliced ham or prosciutto
8 oz. elbow macaroni
3 Tbsp butter
2 Tbsp four
1 1/4 cups whole milk
1 1/2 cups shredded Monterey Jack cheese (about 4 ounces)
3/4 cup shredded sharp Cheddar cheese (about 2 ounces)
Salt and pepper to taste

Directions:
Preheat oven to 350°. Spray two jumbo size muffin tins with non-stick cooking spray. Wrap the slices of ham around the sides and bottom of each muffin cup. Cook pasta according to directions. In a sauté pan, melt the butter and add the flour, stirring until combined completely. Gradually add in the milk and then the cheese, stirring until it melts. Add more milk if needed. Add the cooked pasta to the cheese mixture, stirring well. Spoon into muffin cups and bake for 25-30 minutes.

 Entrees

INDIVIDUAL SPAGHETTI PIES

Ingredients:
1 13 1/2-oz. package angel hair pasta, cooked and drained
2 Tbsp butter
1 cup Parmesan cheese
2 eggs, beaten
1 jar of spaghetti sauce
1 lb. Italian sausage, cooked and grease drained
1 8-oz. package cream cheese
2 cups shredded Mozzarella cheese

Directions:
Preheat oven to 350°. Spray two jumbo size muffin tins with non-stick cooking spray. Melt the butter in the hot pasta, add in the Parmesan cheese and beaten eggs. Mix well. Divide evenly between the muffin cups. Use a spoon to spread the pasta up the sides of the muffin cups. Mix together the spaghetti sauce and the Italian sausage. Put one Tbsp cream cheese into the bottom of each cup and then cover with about 1/3 cup of the spaghetti sauce. Top with mozzarella cheese. Bake 20 minutes or until sauce is bubbly and cheese is melted.

QUICK TUNA-MELT BITES

Ingredients:
Butter
4 slices of hearty whole wheat bread, crusts removed
1 5-oz. can white albacore tuna in water, drained
1–2 stalks celery, chopped fine
1–2 green onions, chopped
2–3 Tbsp mayonnaise or salad dressing
1 ripe avocado, cut into thin slices
4 slices of Muenster, Monterey Jack cheese, or your preference

Directions:
Preheat oven to 350°. Butter both sides of the pieces of bread and then cut them into fourths (quarters). Push each piece of bread into a mini muffin tin cup. In a medium bowl, mix together the tuna, celery, onion, and mayonnaise. Divide evenly among the muffin cups and place one or two slices of avocado on top of each one. Cut the slices of cheese into quarters and put one quarter on the top of each avocado piece. Bake in the oven for 12-15 minutes until bread is toasty and cheese is melted.

# Entrees

SALMON AND GOAT CHEESE FRITTATA SALAD

Ingredients:
Butter, approx. 6 Tbsp, divided
1/2 cup onion, chopped
Salt and pepper to taste
6 oz. fresh mushrooms, sliced thin
3 oz. goat cheese (chevre), crumbled
1/2 cup salmon, cooked and cut in bite size pieces
1 Tbsp whole milk
6 eggs
Fresh salad greens
1/2 cup dried cranberries
Ranch dressing, or dressing of choice

Directions:
Preheat the oven to 350°. Generously coat wells of a standard size (12 well) muffin pan with butter; set aside. Melt 1 Tbsp of butter in a frying pan over medium heat. Add onion and cook until caramelized and golden brown, 20-30 minutes. Watch heat so it doesn't burn. Season with salt and pepper, and transfer mixture to a medium bowl. Add 1 Tbsp butter and sliced mushrooms to the frying pan, season with salt and pepper, and cook until golden brown, about 10 minutes. Add to bowl with the onion. Add crumbled goat cheese and salmon to bowl and stir to evenly combine; set aside. Place eggs and milk in large bowl and whisk until well combined, about 1 minute. Spoon onion-mushroom-cheese mixture evenly among the wells of muffin pan, then fill each almost to the top with egg mixture. Bake until puffed and centers are set, about 12-15 minutes. Remove pan to a wire rack and cool. Meanwhile, place greens on serving plates and sprinkle with dried cranberries. Run a knife around the perimeter of each well to loosen and remove the frittatas. Serve on individual plates with greens and cranberries, with ranch dressing on the side.

CUBAN SLIDERS

Ingredients:
24 pack of sweet dinner rolls (such as Hawaiian)
1 package of sliced ham lunch meat
1 package of 8 slices of Swiss cheese
Dill pickles
1 stick (1/2 cup) of melted butter
2 Tbsp Dijon mustard
1 Tbsp minced onion

Directions:
Preheat oven to 325°. Spray two jumbo size muffin tins
with non-stick cooking spray. Cut the Hawaiian rolls in half
removing the top and placing the bottom of a roll in each
muffin cup. Layer the meat, cheese, and pickles. Place the top
of the rolls on top. Whisk together the butter and the Dijon
mustard. Add in the minced onion and stir. Spoon the Dijon
over the top of the rolls. Cover the muffin tins with foil and
bake for 15 minutes. Remove the foil and continue to bake for
an additional 10 minutes or until the rolls are a toasted brown.

 Entrees

CHINESE NOODLES AND VEGETABLES

Ingredients:
2 Tbsp olive oil
2 cups cooked chicken, diced
2 stalks celery, chopped
1/2 yellow onion, chopped
2 carrots, chopped
1 can bamboo shoots
1 sweet red pepper, chopped
1 cup fresh mushrooms, chopped
1/3 cup slivered almonds, toasted
2 packages chicken flavored ramen noodle soup
1 can crunchy Chinese noodles

Directions:
Preheat oven to 350°. Spray a jumbo size muffin tin with non-stick cooking spray, set aside. In a large frying pan, stir fry the chicken and vegetables in the oil, adding the nuts at the end. In a saucepan, cook the ramen soup for 2 minutes then drain the liquid off the noodles. Divide the noodles between the six cups of the muffin tin. Using your fingers, spread the noodles over the bottom and up the sides of the muffin cups. Spoon the stir fried mixture into the muffin cups. Sprinkle the crunchy Chinese noodles on top and bake for 10 minutes until heated through. Using a spoon, gently lift each noodle cup onto a serving plate.

Entrees

FAMILY HAMBURGER FAVORITE

Ingredients:
1 Tbsp oil
1/2 onion, chopped
1 lb. ground beef
1 can tomato purée
1 cup green beans, cooked tender and cut into 1-inch pieces
2 cups mashed potatoes
1/2 cup Cheddar cheese, shredded

Directions:
Preheat oven to 350°. Sauté the onion in oil in a medium frying pan until tender. In a bowl, combine the ground beef and tomato puree. Add the sautéed onion to the meat mixture. Make a meatball for each muffin cup, large enough so that it can be pressed into the sides and bottom of the muffin cup. Add a spoonful of green beans and a spoonful of mashed potatoes. Top with shredded cheese. Bake for 20 minutes or until hamburger is cooked through. Remove from muffin cup to a paper towel to drain the grease before serving.

MEXICAN CHICKEN PINWHEELS

Ingredients:
1 cup cooked chicken, diced
1 cup Monterey Jack cheese, shredded
5 large flour tortillas
2 Tbsp butter
1 1/2 Tbsp flour
1 cup chicken broth
1/2 cup sour cream
2 4-oz. diced green chiles
Extra shredded cheese for top

Directions:
Preheat oven to 350°. Spray a standard size muffin tin with non-stick cooking spray, set aside. Combine the chicken and cheese. Place one large spoonful of the chicken and cheese mixture onto each tortilla and then rollup. Slice the roll-ups into 3-4 pieces and lay a slice of roll-up flat in the muffin cups. The smaller end pieces can be doubled up in a muffin cup. In a frying pan, melt the butter, stir in the flour and cook over medium heat for a minute or so, stirring constantly. Gradually mix in the broth, whisking until smooth. Stir while sauce is thickening and then add in the sour cream and green chiles. Spoon the sauce over the tortillas in the muffin cups. Top off with more shredded cheese. Bake for 10-12 minutes until cheese has melted.

Entrees

HAM AND TATERS

Ingredients:
3-4 russet potatoes, peeled
1 stick (1/2 cup) butter
1 cup ham, diced
1 cup green onion, chopped
1 cup Monterey Jack cheese, Muenster, or your choice
1 cup heavy cream
Salt and pepper to taste

Directions:
Preheat oven to 350°. Spray a mini muffin tin with non-stick cooking spray, set aside. Using a mandolin slicer, slice the potatoes very thin. Place one pat of butter in each muffin cup. Then layer a small stack of sliced potatoes, salt and pepper to taste, some of the diced ham, a bit of chopped onion, and shredded cheese. Then repeat the layers. Pour the cream over all, then set another pat of butter on the top.

Place in the oven and bake for 15-20 minutes until golden brown and bubbly. Let set in the muffin tin for a couple of minutes before removing to a serving platter.

MUFFIN TIN CALZONES

Ingredients:
1 tube refrigerated pizza dough
Favorite pizza toppings
1 small jar pizza or spaghetti sauce
Mozzarella cheese, shredded
Ranch or marinara sauce for dipping

Directions:
Preheat oven to 350°. Spray a standard or jumbo size muffin tin with non-stick cooking spray. Slice the pizza dough into even amount for the muffin cups, pressing down lightly in the bottom of the cup. Load the dough with your favorite pizza toppings, a spoonful or two of pizza sauce, and the shredded cheese. Pull the edges of the dough up and pinch together at the top. Bake for 15 minutes or until lightly browned. Serve hot with ranch or marinara sauce for dipping.

MAINE CRAB MUFFIN CAKES

Ingredients:
2 (6-oz.) cans crabmeat, drained, flaked
1/2 tsp seafood seasoning
1 Tbsp butter
1/2 cup onion, chopped
1 cup Mozzarella cheese, shredded
1/2 cup biscuit baking mix
1/2 cup milk
2 eggs

Directions:
Heat oven to 375°. Spray 12 standard-size muffin cups with non-stick cooking spray. In small bowl, mix crabmeat and seafood seasoning, set aside. In a medium skillet, sauté onion in butter until tender. Add crabmeat mixture, stirring until mixture is heated through. Cool 5 minutes; stir in cheese.
In a medium bowl, stir biscuit mix, milk and eggs with whisk until blended. Spoon almost 1 Tbsp of the mixture into each muffin cup. Top with about 1/4 cup crab mixture. Spoon another Tbsp biscuit mixture onto crab mixture in each muffin cup. Bake about 30 minutes or until toothpick inserted in center comes out clean and tops are golden brown. Cool 5-10 minutes before removing.

 Entrees

RESTAURANT STYLE TACO SALAD BOWLS

Ingredients:
6 small flour tortillas
Canola oil spray
1 lb. ground beef
1 package taco seasoning
1 can kidney beans
1 bag of shredded iceberg lettuce
Cheddar cheese, grated
Grape tomatoes, sliced
Avocado, sliced
Sour cream

Directions:
Preheat the oven to 375°. Using two muffin tin pans, spray the inside of one pan with non-stick cooking spray and the backside of the other. Warm the tortillas slightly in the microwave so they are flexible and then fit the tortillas into the muffin cups and by gently pleating the tortilla edges, pushing down till they fit. Set the top pan on top of the first one and press down lightly to mold the tortillas. Bake for 14-16 minutes or until the edges start to turn golden brown and the tortillas become crispy. Remove from the oven and let the shells cool on a wire rack. Meanwhile, in a skillet, scramble the ground beef, adding the seasoning when almost cooked. Drain the grease. Mix in the kidney beans. Put a large spoonful of the hamburger mixture into each tortilla shell topping with some lettuce, cheese, tomatoes, avocado, and sour cream.

FANCY POTATOES

Ingredients:
Unsalted butter, melted
2-4 medium russet potatoes
Salt and pepper to taste
3/4 cup cream

Directions:
Preheat oven to 400°. Brush 6 standard size muffin cups with butter. Slice potatoes very thin. Place 2 slices in each cup and season with salt and pepper. Continue adding potatoes, seasoning every few slices, until cups are filled. Pour 2 tablespoons of heavy cream over each. Bake until potatoes are golden brown and tender when pierced with a knife, 30 to 35 minutes. Remove from oven and run a knife under and around the potatoes. Spoon the individual servings onto a platter.

 Sides

HASH BROWN CUPS

Ingredients:
1 large pkg frozen hash browns (32-oz.)
1 can cream of chicken soup
2 cups sour cream
3/4 cup butter, melted
2 Tbsp onion, chopped
2 cups shredded Cheddar cheese
2 cups flaked corn cereal, crushed

Directions:
Preheat oven to 350°. Spray standard size muffin tin with non-stick cooking spray. Thaw and drain hash browns, pressing excess water out if necessary. In a large mixing bowl combine the soup, sour cream, butter, onion and cheddar cheese. Add in the hash browns. Place one heaping spoonful of the hash brown mixture into each muffin cup. Sprinkle crushed cereal on top. Bake for 30 minutes or until potatoes are tender. Let the potatoes set for about 10 minutes before turning them out onto a serving platter.

Sides

BACON AND TOMATO PUDDING BITES

Ingredients:
1 stick (1/2 cup) butter
2 cups bread crumbs, crushed
1 10 1/2-oz. can tomato puree
1 cup brown sugar
1/4 cup water
1/4 tsp salt
4 slices of bacon, cooked and cut into small pieces

Directions:
Preheat oven to 325°. Spray mini muffin tin with non-stick cooking spray. Melt the butter and pour over the bread crumbs, mixing well. In a small saucepan, add the rest of the ingredients, except bacon. Bring to a simmer, stirring for 5 minutes. Pour the tomato mixture over the bread crumbs and stir. Spoon into mini muffin cups, filling about 2/3 full. Top each with bacon pieces. Cover the muffin tin with foil. Bake for 30 minutes.

Sides

NEW MEXICO RICE AND GREEN CHILES

Ingredients:
3 cups rice, cooked
1 cup sour cream
1 cup Cheddar cheese, shredded
2 cups cottage cheese
1 4-oz. can diced green chiles

Directions:
Preheat oven to 350°. Spray mini muffin tin with non-stick cooking spray. Mix all ingredients together and spoon into muffin cups. Top with additional shredded cheese. Bake for 25-30 minutes.

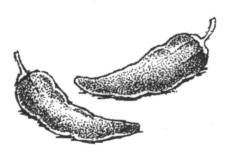

 Sides

OLD WORLD MEXICAN SPOON BREAD

Ingredients:
1 stick (1/2 cup) butter, cut into tablespoons
3 eggs, beaten
1 package corn muffin mix
1 can cream-style corn
1 can corn
1 cup sour cream
1 4-oz. can green chiles, drained (optional)
2 cups cheese, grated, divided

Directions:
Preheat oven to 350°. Spray a standard size muffin tin with non-stick cooking spray, then put the pats of butter into each muffin tin cup. Put the muffin tin in the oven to melt the butter. While the butter melts, in a medium bowl, beat the eggs and add the rest of the ingredients *except* for 1/2 cup of the cheese. Remove the muffin tin from the oven and pour the mixture into each cup, dividing evenly. Sprinkle the reserved 1/2 cup cheese on the tops. Bake for about 35 minutes until golden brown and toothpick inserted in center comes out clean.

Sides

MAKE-AHEAD PARTY FRUIT SLUSH

Ingredients:
2 1/2 cups fruit flavored sparkling soda
1/2 cup sugar
1 can frozen orange juice concentrate, thawed
1/2 cup frozen lemonade concentrate, thawed
4 bananas, sliced
1 can (29-oz.) sliced peaches, undrained and chopped
1 can (20-oz.) pineapple chunks, undrained
1 can (15-oz.) mandarin oranges, drained
1 package (10-oz.) frozen sweetened sliced strawberries,
   thawed
3/4 cup blueberries, washed
Lettuce leaves
Mint leaves for garnish

Directions:
In a large bowl, combine all ingredients. Spoon into standard size muffin tins. Freeze 8 hours or overnight. Remove from freezer an hour before serving. Serve on a bed of lettuce with a mint leaf garnish.

Makes about 4 dozen frozen slushes—an easy and cool make-ahead dish for a crowd!

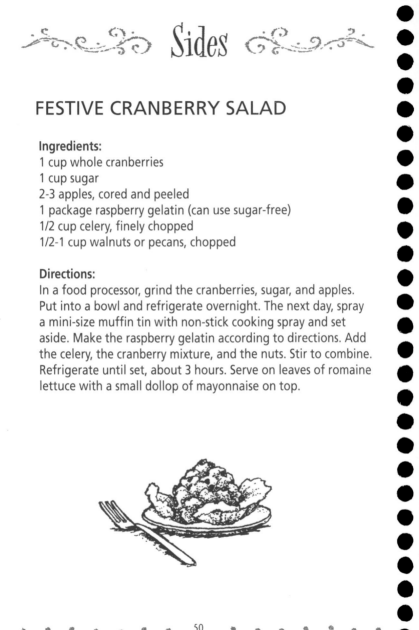

Sides

FESTIVE CRANBERRY SALAD

Ingredients:
1 cup whole cranberries
1 cup sugar
2-3 apples, cored and peeled
1 package raspberry gelatin (can use sugar-free)
1/2 cup celery, finely chopped
1/2-1 cup walnuts or pecans, chopped

Directions:
In a food processor, grind the cranberries, sugar, and apples. Put into a bowl and refrigerate overnight. The next day, spray a mini-size muffin tin with non-stick cooking spray and set aside. Make the raspberry gelatin according to directions. Add the celery, the cranberry mixture, and the nuts. Stir to combine. Refrigerate until set, about 3 hours. Serve on leaves of romaine lettuce with a small dollop of mayonnaise on top.

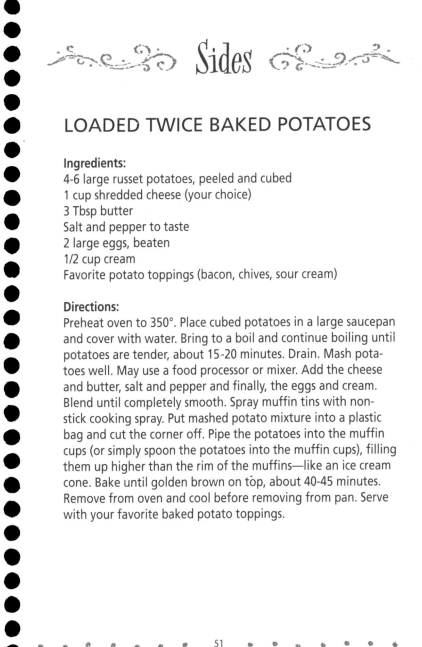

Sides

LOADED TWICE BAKED POTATOES

Ingredients:
4-6 large russet potatoes, peeled and cubed
1 cup shredded cheese (your choice)
3 Tbsp butter
Salt and pepper to taste
2 large eggs, beaten
1/2 cup cream
Favorite potato toppings (bacon, chives, sour cream)

Directions:
Preheat oven to 350°. Place cubed potatoes in a large saucepan and cover with water. Bring to a boil and continue boiling until potatoes are tender, about 15-20 minutes. Drain. Mash potatoes well. May use a food processor or mixer. Add the cheese and butter, salt and pepper and finally, the eggs and cream. Blend until completely smooth. Spray muffin tins with non-stick cooking spray. Put mashed potato mixture into a plastic bag and cut the corner off. Pipe the potatoes into the muffin cups (or simply spoon the potatoes into the muffin cups), filling them up higher than the rim of the muffins—like an ice cream cone. Bake until golden brown on top, about 40-45 minutes. Remove from oven and cool before removing from pan. Serve with your favorite baked potato toppings.

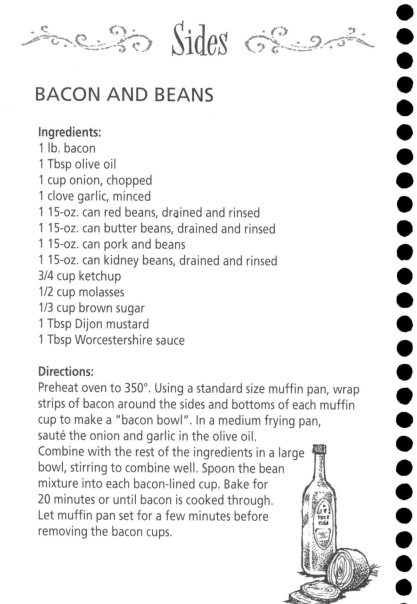

Sides

BACON AND BEANS

Ingredients:
1 lb. bacon
1 Tbsp olive oil
1 cup onion, chopped
1 clove garlic, minced
1 15-oz. can red beans, drained and rinsed
1 15-oz. can butter beans, drained and rinsed
1 15-oz. can pork and beans
1 15-oz. can kidney beans, drained and rinsed
3/4 cup ketchup
1/2 cup molasses
1/3 cup brown sugar
1 Tbsp Dijon mustard
1 Tbsp Worcestershire sauce

Directions:
Preheat oven to 350°. Using a standard size muffin pan, wrap strips of bacon around the sides and bottoms of each muffin cup to make a "bacon bowl". In a medium frying pan, sauté the onion and garlic in the olive oil. Combine with the rest of the ingredients in a large bowl, stirring to combine well. Spoon the bean mixture into each bacon-lined cup. Bake for 20 minutes or until bacon is cooked through. Let muffin pan set for a few minutes before removing the bacon cups.

Sides

BUTTERY BROCCOLI-CAULIFLOWER BITES

Ingredients:
2 Tbsp butter
1 cup broccoli, coarsely chopped
1 cup cauliflower, coarsely chopped
1/3 cup Cheddar cheese, shredded
2 Tbsp bread crumbs
1/2 tsp seasoning salt
Black pepper to taste
1 egg, beaten
Extra butter for the tops

Directions:
Preheat oven to 400°. Spray a mini muffin pan with non-stick spray. Melt the butter in a skillet and then sauté the vegetables in the butter until tender but not soft.

Using a food processor, finely chop the broccoli and cauliflower. Don't over chop—the vegetables should be fine but not puréed. In a medium bowl stir together the vegetables, Cheddar cheese, bread crumbs, and seasonings. Add the beaten egg and stir until the ingredients are moistened with egg. Spoon 1 Tbsp of the vegetable mixture into each mini muffin cup and top with a dab of butter. Bake 15 minutes. Remove muffin pan from oven and turn the Broccoli-Cauliflower Bites over so the bottoms can brown. Bake another 15 minutes. Serve immediately.

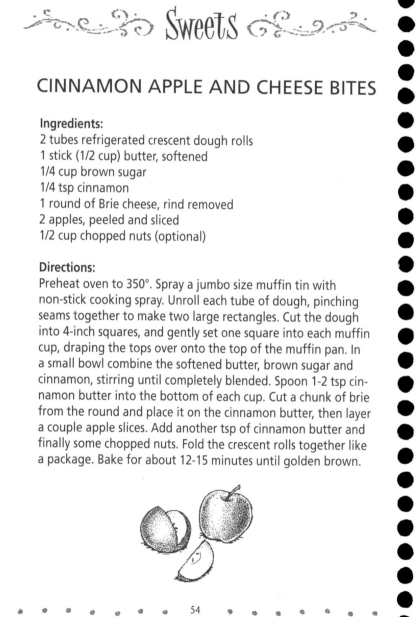

Sweets

CINNAMON APPLE AND CHEESE BITES

Ingredients:
2 tubes refrigerated crescent dough rolls
1 stick (1/2 cup) butter, softened
1/4 cup brown sugar
1/4 tsp cinnamon
1 round of Brie cheese, rind removed
2 apples, peeled and sliced
1/2 cup chopped nuts (optional)

Directions:
Preheat oven to 350°. Spray a jumbo size muffin tin with non-stick cooking spray. Unroll each tube of dough, pinching seams together to make two large rectangles. Cut the dough into 4-inch squares, and gently set one square into each muffin cup, draping the tops over onto the top of the muffin pan. In a small bowl combine the softened butter, brown sugar and cinnamon, stirring until completely blended. Spoon 1-2 tsp cinnamon butter into the bottom of each cup. Cut a chunk of brie from the round and place it on the cinnamon butter, then layer a couple apple slices. Add another tsp of cinnamon butter and finally some chopped nuts. Fold the crescent rolls together like a package. Bake for about 12-15 minutes until golden brown.

UPSIDE-DOWN OATMEAL CAKE

Ingredients:

2 sticks of butter, softened to room temperature
1 cup quick cooking oats
1 cup boiling water
1/2 cup maple syrup
3/4 cup brown sugar
1 cup coconut
1/4 cup chopped pecans
1/4 tsp vanilla
2 Tbsp granulated sugar
2 Tbsp brown sugar
2 Tbsp flour
1/4 tsp baking soda
1/2 tsp cinnamon
1/8 tsp nutmeg
1/8 tsp ginger
2 eggs, beaten
Vanilla ice cream

Directions:

Preheat oven to 350°. Spray a standard size muffin tin with non-stick cooking spray. Mix together one stick of butter, oats and boiling water. Set aside. Spoon 1 Tbsp maple syrup into the bottom of each muffin tin. In a medium bowl, add the other stick of softened butter, brown sugar, coconut, and pecans. Stir in vanilla. Put a heaping spoonful of this mixture on top of the maple syrup in each tin. In a mixing bowl, combine the granulated sugar, brown sugar, flour, baking soda, spices and eggs. Add the oatmeal mixture into the sugar/flour mixture. Stir just to combine and pour this batter into the muffin tins, filling 2/3 full. Bake for 25-30 minutes or until a toothpick inserted into center of each cupcake comes out clean. Using extreme caution to avoid burns, immediately place a platter upside-down on top of the muffin tin and flip the entire tin over onto the platter. The sauce will be bubbly hot so be careful! Enjoy with a spoonful of vanilla ice cream.

Sweets

FRENCH PEARS IN PASTRY WITH MAPLE-GINGER CREAM

Ingredients:

1/2 cup pure maple syrup
1/2 tsp fresh ginger root, peeled and grated/zested
3 Tbsp butter
1/3 cup light brown sugar
2 Tbsp candied or crystallized ginger, finely chopped
1/8 tsp salt

1/4 cup golden raisins
1/3 cup walnuts, toasted and coarsely chopped
2 Bartlett or Anjou pears, peeled and sliced very thin
2 tubes crescent roll dough
3/4 cup very cold heavy cream
1/4 cup brown sugar

Directions:

Preheat oven to 350°. Spray standard size muffin tin with non-stick cooking spray. Pour maple syrup into small saucepan and add fresh ginger root. Bring to a simmer, then remove from heat and let cool. Melt butter in frying pan, add brown sugar, candied or crystallized ginger, salt, raisins and walnuts. Cook over medium heat 2-3 minutes. Add pears to brown sugar mixture, and cook another 2-3 minutes. Remove from heat and cool to room temperature. Meanwhile, unroll dough, keep seams intact, pinching together where necessary to make one large rectangle with each tube of dough. Spoon cooled pears over top of dough evenly. Beginning on short end of dough, roll entire rectangle into one fat tube. Do same with second roll of dough. Cut dough into rounds and place each into a muffin cup. Bake for 12-15 minutes or until golden brown. Meanwhile, using mixer, whip cream, adding in brown sugar, until stiff peaks form. Turn mixer to low speed and drizzle maple-ginger syrup into whipped cream. Before serving the pastries, put a dollop of Maple-Ginger Cream on top of each.

CRISPY APPLE TARTS

Ingredients:
1/2 tsp cinnamon
3/4 cup granulated sugar
1/4 cup light brown sugar
1/2 cup rolled oats
3/4 cup flour
1/4 tsp salt
1 stick (1/2 cup) butter, softened
5 cups peeled, cored, sliced apples or canned apples
  (not pie filling)
Vanilla ice cream

Directions:
Preheat oven to 350°. Spray a standard size muffin tin with non-stick cooking spray. In a mixing bowl, combine the first seven ingredients. Add the butter and mix until well distributed. Put 1-2 heaping Tbsps of the butter/oats mixture into each of the prepared muffin cups. Using your fingers, press the mixture into the bottom and sides of each cup. Spoon about 1/4 cup apples into each muffin cup and then cover with more of the crumble mix. Bake for about 30 minutes or until apples are fork tender. Remove with a large spoon and serve with vanilla ice cream.

WHITE CHOCOLATE RASPBERRY CUSTARD

Ingredients:
1/2 cup sugar
3 Tbsp cornstarch
1/2 tsp salt
3 cups whole milk
4 egg yolks
1 tsp vanilla
1 cup white chocolate chips
1/2 stick (1/4 cup) unsalted butter, cut into pieces
Fresh raspberries

Directions:
In a heavy large sauce pan, whisk together the sugar, cornstarch and salt. Put on medium-high heat. Immediately add the milk and yolks, whisking to blend. Continue to whisk while the liquid is heating up for 10 to 15 minutes. Once it starts to thicken and bubble, turn off burner and take the pan off the heat. Slowly add the vanilla, white chocolate chips, and cold butter pieces, continuing to stir. Once the butter and white chocolate have melted, pour into standard size muffin tin cups and cover with plastic wrap—make sure the wrap is touching the custard on the top so that a skin does not form. Refrigerate until cooled or overnight. Remove the plastic wrap and invert the muffin tin onto a serving platter and move them to individual serving dishes if desired. Top with fresh raspberries and shaved white chocolate pieces.

Sweets

MUFFIN TIN MUD PIES

Ingredients:
1 package original chocolate sandwich cookies
2 Tbsp butter, melted
1 container coffee flavored ice cream
Chocolate syrup
Whipped cream (optional)

Directions:
Place 1 chocolate cookie half on the bottom of each muffin tin cup. Place about 6-8 cookies in a gallon size zip-lock bag and seal. Crush the cookies into crumbs, inside frosting and all. Add the melted butter and blend with the crumbs. Place one large spoonful of the crumbs in each muffin cup and press around the sides. Soften (but don't melt) the ice cream and spoon into each muffin cup. Cover the top with more cookie crumbs. Put in the freezer for at least 3 hours. Remove carefully. Drizzle chocolate syrup on top and add a dollop of whipped cream before serving.

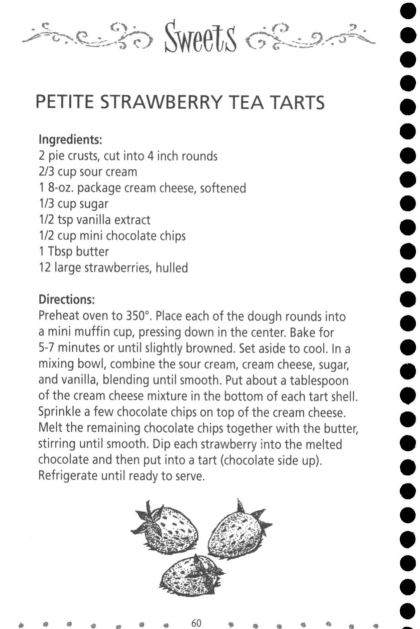

Sweets

PETITE STRAWBERRY TEA TARTS

Ingredients:
2 pie crusts, cut into 4 inch rounds
2/3 cup sour cream
1 8-oz. package cream cheese, softened
1/3 cup sugar
1/2 tsp vanilla extract
1/2 cup mini chocolate chips
1 Tbsp butter
12 large strawberries, hulled

Directions:
Preheat oven to 350°. Place each of the dough rounds into a mini muffin cup, pressing down in the center. Bake for 5-7 minutes or until slightly browned. Set aside to cool. In a mixing bowl, combine the sour cream, cream cheese, sugar, and vanilla, blending until smooth. Put about a tablespoon of the cream cheese mixture in the bottom of each tart shell. Sprinkle a few chocolate chips on top of the cream cheese. Melt the remaining chocolate chips together with the butter, stirring until smooth. Dip each strawberry into the melted chocolate and then put into a tart (chocolate side up). Refrigerate until ready to serve.

CHOCOLATE CHIP MINI CHEESECAKES

Ingredients:
2 cups graham cracker crumbs
2 Tbsp sugar
6 Tbsp butter, melted
2 (8-oz.) package cream cheese, softened
1/2 cup powdered sugar
2 large eggs
1/4 cup heavy whipping cream
1 tsp vanilla extract
1 cup mini chocolate chips

Directions:
Preheat oven to 325°. In a bowl, stir together the graham
cracker crumbs, sugar, and melted butter and then spoon into
the cups of a mini muffin tin. Pat and press onto the bottom
and sides of each cup using your fingers or a spoon, until a
fairly sturdy crust has formed on the sides. Put in the freezer
while preparing the filling. Using an electric mixer, combine
the cream cheese and powdered sugar for 3 minutes. Add the
eggs, one at a time, and then the cream and vanilla. Beat on
medium-high for 3-4 minutes. Fold the mini chocolate chips
into the mixture. Remove the muffin tin from the freezer and
pour the cream cheese mixture into each crust. Bake for 35
minutes or until tops are set. Refrigerate before serving.

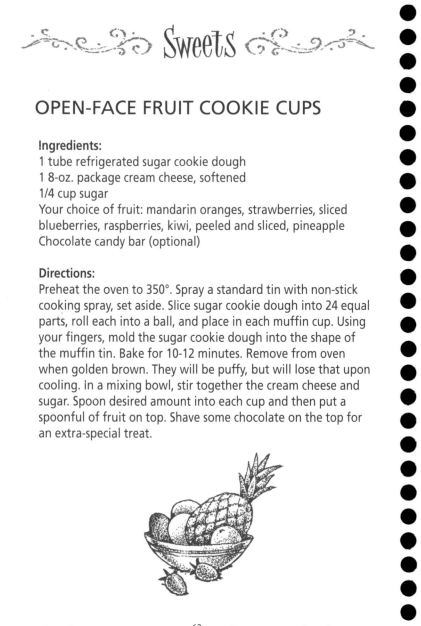

Sweets

OPEN-FACE FRUIT COOKIE CUPS

Ingredients:
1 tube refrigerated sugar cookie dough
1 8-oz. package cream cheese, softened
1/4 cup sugar
Your choice of fruit: mandarin oranges, strawberries, sliced
blueberries, raspberries, kiwi, peeled and sliced, pineapple
Chocolate candy bar (optional)

Directions:
Preheat the oven to 350°. Spray a standard tin with non-stick
cooking spray, set aside. Slice sugar cookie dough into 24 equal
parts, roll each into a ball, and place in each muffin cup. Using
your fingers, mold the sugar cookie dough into the shape of
the muffin tin. Bake for 10-12 minutes. Remove from oven
when golden brown. They will be puffy, but will lose that upon
cooling. In a mixing bowl, stir together the cream cheese and
sugar. Spoon desired amount into each cup and then put a
spoonful of fruit on top. Shave some chocolate on the top for
an extra-special treat.

LAYERED COCONUT COOKIES

Ingredients:
2 cups flaked coconut
1/2 stick (1/4 cup) butter, softened
1/2 cup pecans, chopped
1 cup semisweet chocolate chips
1 cup butterscotch chips
1 1/2 cups graham cracker crumbs
1 14-oz. can sweetened condensed milk

Directions:
Preheat oven to 350°. In a bowl, combine the coconut and butter. Divide into the cups of a standard size muffin tin and then press into the sides and bottom of each cup to form the crust. Bake for 10 minutes. Remove from the oven. Layer the pecans, chocolate chips, butterscotch chips, and graham cracker butter mixture between the muffin cups, dividing evenly. Pour the condensed milk over the layers and then generously sprinkle the graham cracker mixture over all. Bake for 15 minutes.

Sweets

VANILLA-TOFFEE MINI CHEESECAKES

Ingredients:
1 cup plus 2 Tbsp crushed toffee/coconut flavored sandwich
    cookie crumbs (scrape off the filling and discard)
1 Tbsp butter, melted
1 8-oz. pkg cream cheese
1 egg
1/4 cup sugar
1/2 tsp vanilla extract

Directions:
Spray a standard size muffin tin with non-stick cooking spray.
In a small bowl, mix together the cookie crumbs and the
melted butter. Divide the crumble evenly among the muffin tin
cups, reserving some for topping. Pressing down with a spoon
or your fingers to make a crust. In a mixing bowl, blend the
cream cheese, egg, sugar and vanilla until smooth. Spoon over
the cookie crusts to almost fill each muffin cup. Bake for 25-30
minutes or until centers are nearly set. Sprinkle more cookie
crumbs on the tops.